Carlo Carrà
Works on Paper
Estorick Collection London
10 October 2001 - 20 January 2002

Exhibition curated by
Massimo Carrà and Renato Miracco

Ministry of Foreign Affairs, Rome
Cultural Promotion and Cooperation Department

Francesco Aloisi de Larderel
Director General

Francesca Tardioli
Head of Office II (Cultural Events)

Alessandro Nigro
Head of Modern Art Exhibitions Division, Office II

Exhibition organised by
Alessandro Nigro, Ministry of Foreign Affairs, Rome
Roberta Cremoncini, Estorick Collection, London

Special thanks to the **Italian Cultural Institute** in London for their contribution
towards this publication.

Acknowledgments
Massimo and Cornelia Carrà, Luca Carrà, Giorgio Chierici, Antonio and Marina
Forchino, Lodovico Isolabella, Giulio Maira, Carla Mazzoni, Gabriele and Bianca
Mazzotta, Giovanni and Liliana Pandini, Elio Pinottini, Daniele and Giovanna
Sette, Galleria Anna D'Ascanio (Rome), Galleria Pegaso (Forte dei Marmi),
Galleria La Scaletta (San Polo d'Enza).
Courier Department, Ministry of Foreign Affairs, Rome (Marina Simeoni Poli and
Gianfranco Castellani), Assitalia insurance company, AEIA transport company.

Estorick Collection
of modern italian art

Carlo Carrà

Works on Paper

Mazzotta

Photographic credits
Studio fotografico Luca Carrà
Archivio Fondazione Mazzotta

Translation
Chris Adams

© 2001 Edizioni Gabriele Mazzotta
Foro Buonaparte 52 - 20121 Milano

ISBN 88-202-1505-5

Printed in Italy

Carlo Carrà's work is a pivotal reference point in the history of 20th century Italian culture. As an artist Carrà underwent an extraordinary journey of stylistic evolution; in his youth he was at the forefront of the first dynamic impulse of Futurism.

He explored the ideological and artistic possibilities of the movement in six fruitful years, only to radically shift his focus in 1917 and engage with the Metaphysical style established by Giorgio de Chirico. By 1920 Carrà was writing theoretical discourses in the review Valori Plastici *and in his artistic practice he moved towards a more historicist view, producing works full of allusions to an Italian tradition in the visual arts. His mature works are characterised by a return to classical frames of reference.*

This retrospective of 120 Carrà drawings is a marvellous opportunity to look at the richness and diversity in one artist's career, and the exhibition would not have been possible without loans from many Italian private collections. The Estorick Collection is indebted to all the lenders and, in particular, Massimo Carrà for his major contribution to this exhibition. I would like to thank H.E. the Italian Ambassador, Signor Luigi Amaduzzi, the Cultural Promotion an Cooperation Department of the Ministry of Foreign Affairs in Rome, and in particular Ambassador Francesco Aloisi de Larderel and Francesca Tardioli for making this project possible, Alessandro Nigro for organising the exhibition and Renato Miracco for co-curating the exhibiton with Massimo Carrà. As ever, Roberta Cremoncini, our curator, has been tireless
in making preparations for the London showing.

Alexandra Noble
Director, Estorick Collection

Contents

Drawing as a Mental Laboratory

Massimo Carrà

Alongside painting Carrà always devoted much attention to drawing, making it a daily activity which has left us a *corpus* of thousands of pieces, reflecting the entire arc of his work in its exploration of different aesthetic vocabularies. The reason for this is that by its very nature drawing – a true mental laboratory – allowed him that spontaneity and immediacy of execution best suited to expressing an emergent idea, even when not yet fully formed. Sketches, notes, annotations in pencil or ink enabled the painter to clarify – without filters or veils – an intuition or a desire for formal experimentation, in sight of a possible image yet to find resolution in the context of an eventual new formal system. And this was true of either a preparatory study for an already projected pictorial work or one conceived of as an end in itself, a self-sufficient expression of a particular stage in his aesthetic thought. And, in the one case as in the other, the page was understood as an atmospheric space to be animated by a patient modelling of forms, expressed solely through the values of the line, the sign and the rhythms of black and white.

For Carrà, art could never simply be the result of an instinctive impulse, of a fleeting sensation, nor was it a matter of sensibility or emotion: rather, art was an attempt to grasp the complex and always slightly mysterious relationship between things in their reality and the intervention of the artist who, through a mental operation, is able to detach them from their contingency, from their phenomenal existence, in order to purify them and re-present them in accordance with an "absolute" vision. Art, that is to say, was understood not as a means of reproducing the physical appearance of reality, but rather of creating a "new thing", an entity reflective of the complex and profound relationship between the individual and the external world, outside of any representative anecdote.

Pursuing this principle, Carrà's research, both as a draughtsman and as a painter, was oriented to the simplest, most unadorned representation of the image so as to form out of this its secret essence. This research followed a line of continuity which naturally did not exclude but, on the contrary, gradually postulated different forms and expressive vocabularies. A denuded image thus prevails, oriented toward an ideal target of absolute form – that is to say, the image fully resolved in a formal theorem – or else a more cursive discourse, one closer to the immediacy of the primary emotion. On one occasion the line may be dry and harsh; on another, softer, more pictorial.

In drawing, as in painting, the constant point of departure was observation from real life, in order to gather from it the immediate impulses and the emotional values, after which there followed a patient mental re-elaboration in the realms of memory and imagination: two distinct phases, but ones destined to blend into one another in a process of synthesis, with the aim of attaining that difficult equilibrium between the concrete element (the thing in its reality) and its transfiguration or abstraction, which was always the central problem of Carrà's work. He conceived of "truth", therefore, as a simple starting point and stimulus to the pictorial imagination, always to be verified with a later, and therefore sufficiently detached meditation.

Perhaps even more than his painting, Carrà's drawing demonstrates in a peremptory manner his rejection of any virtuosity, of any over-refinement or ornamental indulgence. In their place one finds a nudity of language which accompanies every formal inquiry, every experimentation.

As the principal tool in his aesthetic and formal investigations, Carrà's drawing reveals to us the secret process of transposition between the external world and the spirit of the artist, between perception, consciousness and judgement. For him, therefore, drawing represented an ongoing "logbook', a "laboratory notebook" in which to experiment with and realize all the structural, intuitive, semantic, ideographical, symbolic and representative possibilities of the sign.

Mutations of the Spirit

Renato Miracco

Carrà and the Italian cultural climate at the beginning of the twentieth century

"Every adventurous initiative was stifled at birth. Italian artists existed in a state of blind ignorance of the artistic renovation which had been taking place in Europe for several years... The docile admiration for a nauseating, superficial virtuosity prevailed everywhere... Indifference toward developments elsewhere was widely confused with love of our own tradition."

This declaration of Carrà's is symptomatic of a cultural climate characterised by Gino Severini at around the same time in the following manner: "The state of Italian painting at that time was one of the muddiest and most injurious imaginable. Under such conditions, even a Raphael would have had difficulty painting a good picture."

The only innovatory impulse – and one of the fundamental aesthetic sources Futurism was to draw on – was provided by Divisionism, which emerged in Italy in the wake of French Impressionism in 1890 and survived, in various modified forms, until 1915.

Carrà discovered Divisionism during these early years, and became fascinated by it. However, he was not immediately ready to fully absorb its technical lessons, a fact to which many of his paintings executed before 1905 testify.

Besides the Divisionists, Carrà was inspired by the work of Renoir, Cézanne, Pissarro, Sisley, Monet and Gauguin, which he discovered at the Musée du Luxembourg in Paris, as well as that of Constable and Turner, which he saw at London's National Gallery.

At this time he became greatly preoccupied with a question which began to be considered on a wide scale during those years: "Today, it is necessary to confront the issue of the relationship between art and its environment." Tolstoy's text *What is Art?* was published in 1899 and contained statements such as: "The individual is the product of the environment in which he lives" and "The artist is the individual who proposes examples in order to improve social conditions."

One can perceive echoes of these theories in the ideas of the Divisionist painter Pellizza da Volpedo, when he asserts: "I believe this is not an age suited to the ethos of 'art for art's sake', but rather 'art for humanity's sake'." Carrà's reading of Faurier, Owen, Bakunin, Engels and Marx undoubtedly strengthened his convictions about socially committed painting.

The Futurist experience

"It was in February 1910 that Boccioni, Russolo and I met Marinetti... After a lengthy examination of the prevailing artistic climate we decided to launch a manifesto to young Italian artists, urging them to shake off lethargy. My collaboration with the Futurists lasted six years – from the movement's inception in 1910 until 1915. At a time when gentler spirits considered our efforts to be in vain my friends and I were convinced that, on the contrary, the hour had arrived to put aside scepticism and work in a more lively and vigorous manner than ever before."

The period during which Carrà participated in the Futurist movement was experienced by the painter with an intensity which had, as he himself recalled, "something savage and heroic about it".

During these years he managed for the first time to express his theories pictorially with force and determination, and became one of the most important theoreticians of the Italian Futurist movement. For Carrà it was a time of extreme dialectics, constructed and founded on his relationship with Marinetti and Boccioni. In fact, from the very beginning there were two currents and modes of thought, two "souls" within the movement, which were sometimes antithetical (such as after the death of Boccioni) and sometimes complementary. For Boccioni, as for Marinetti, Futurism was a way of understanding life in its totality. For Carrà, it offered a vocabulary promoting the realisation of a "dynamic" mode of painting, directed toward a formal, synthetic solution, the ultimate goal of which was the new architectonic construction of the artwork.

In addition to this it was "a way of shaking public opinion, of entering into more immediate contact with the people… These bizarre mass meetings, addressing artistic problems of which the vast majority of the audience were absolutely ignorant, were necessary and useful, because they aroused an awareness of the need for a full spiritual liberty in a more lively and penetrating manner".

A constant feature of the Futurist writings of Carrà and Boccioni is their need to distinguish their own work from that of the Cubists. However, this was an unnecessary obsession. In fact, whereas Cubism was a revolutionary school of painting, Futurism was a movement which did not restrict itself in this manner but, on the contrary, transformed life into art, and vice versa. A statement concerning the Cubists by Carrà illuminates his evolutionary process of working for us: "The Cubists, in order to be objective, limit themselves to considering objects by moving around them, so as to obtain a geometric schema. We Futurists, on the other hand, strive to insert ourselves into the centre of things through the force of intuition, in such a way that our ego forms a single complex with their uniqueness."

One of Carrà's undoubted contributions to Futurism is that of the onomatopoeic writings which are a feature of his pictorial compositions during this period, where the writing itself, as a simple sign, participates in the architectonic and spatial construction of the image.

The break with the Futurist movement

"In the soul a command rang out, and we attempted once more to recall our miraculously enduring nostalgia."

A careful consideration of the ideas elaborated by Carrà between 1913 and 1915 – that is, at the height of his commitment to Futurism – reveals that they contained all the seeds of his alienation from the movement. The reasons for it were innumerable, but it is possible to document them by reading and comparing his autobiography with his writings and with the letters he sent at this time to his friend and colleague Ardengo Soffici, his inseparable *alter ego* in the new artistic theories which were in the process of forming.

Already by 1913 Carrà had found himself to be in disagreement with the materialistic objectivism of the Cubists, which "sees everything and feels nothing".

The turning point came in 1914. During that year Carrà made another extended visit to Paris which reawakened in him the confrontation with the Cubists to such an extent that a few months later, in the article *Modern life and popular art* (*Vita moderna e arte popolare*), he was to write: "Thank God Cubism is now dead, just as Fauvism and Synthetism died before it… In my opinion, the fundamental explanation for this artistic massacre lies in the fact that all art which is constructed on intellectual and cerebral foundations cannot last long. We Futurists are now convinced that only by working the twofold mine of modern life and popular art would they have been able to discover our origins and realize those new aesthetic values which answer the great needs of our spirit that desires, at any cost, to create a modern primordialism."

To this end Carrà began studying the work of Giotto and Uccello, with the profound desire and intention to identify his own work with history, attempting to recuperate the golden age of Italian art by building a bridge between modernity and the past. "In the magical silence of Giotto's forms our contemplation rests, ecstasy germinates and, little by little, resolves itself in the uncluttered soul."

Carrà progressively abandoned the dynamic, deconstructive vocabulary typical of Futurism, turning instead toward a figurative style characterized by a plastic and iconographical primitivism. This led him further toward that anti-graceful aesthetic which, in actual fact, had been an element of Futurist ideology. On 30 April he wrote to Soffici: "I believe the law of deconstruction has been overcome. Systematic deconstruction has, I find, become a formula to be denied. Naturally enough, Boccioni does not approve of this latest conception of ours. All the worse for him. Let us hope that he too will soon understand the direction in which I am now heading and abandon the cerebral art that fascinates him so much."

In this new spirit Carrà produced many collages in 1915 which were completely different from those of the Futurist period and certainly not Cubist in style. Their difference consists in the fact that for the Cubists, collage was a form of *papier collé* developed in a purely decorative direction, whilst for the Futurists it constituted an "anti-pictorial" element – that is to say, substitutive with regard to colour. Carrà, meanwhile, constructs a variety of collage transcending both typologies to create a third: "In my most recent work I have applied coloured cardboard forms in relief. I find this method of introducing forms in relief satisfying, as it endows the entire work with an industrial quality which leads me away from 'museum art'."

The subject of *The flask* (*Il fiasco*) of 1915 is the intimate relationship that exists between the two objects depicted. Unlike in a Cubist painting the consistency and coexistence of a glass and a bottle is of a purely mental nature. In the use of materials Carrà is faithful to the multi-material aesthetic of Boccioni, who told a friend entrusted with finding such elements for a Futurist exhibition: "I advise you to select highly advanced items, as grotesque and shocking as possible."

But Futurist experimentation, despite its fascinating principles, no longer satisfied Carrà. Recalling those years in his autobiography, he stated: "During the Futurist period I considered any attitude approaching mysticism to be negative for art, whereas now I ask myself whether it was true that mysticism, as an aesthetic doctrine and state of mind, was in contrast with the modern spirit… No personal disagreement drove me to break with Futurism. If, then, I raised up an image of art different from that of Futurism it was in order to better define the new aspiration which was in the process of taking shape in my spirit."

Carrà and Metaphysical Painting

"In December 1916 I published my *Discourse on Giotto* and *Paolo Uccello, constructor* (*Parlata su Giotto* e *Paolo Uccello costruttore*) in *La Voce*. With such texts as these I intervened in the debate on problems of tradition in the modern sense… I can say, without exaggerating, that I had a truly troubled conscience or, so to speak, a fear of advancing… What counts is not the renunciation of a given aesthetic doctrine, but the expansion of our spiritual personality."

Carrà's study of the primitive Italian artistic tradition through the work of Giotto and Uccello thus represented a starting point for him to explore his inner self and, maieutically, bring to light something buried and forgotten.

Alongside this "interior research", the work of Henri Rousseau, which Carrà had seen in Paris, also constituted an iconographical reference point. He admired his partly resolved "anti-graceful ideal" and "what an exquisite instinct and a fervid fantasy can create… Everything has become as it was in primordial times. And, with Henri Rousseau, I will forge the new European painting. To stop myself halfway would seem like a betrayal".

In the meantime, the First World War had broken out and Carrà, not being entirely committed to that Futurist interventionism forming the basis of the manifesto *The Futurist reconstruction of the universe* (*Ricostruzione futurista dell'universo*), written by Balla and Depero in 1915, asserted: "For me, love of the fatherland was a moral entity not to be considered as an abstraction, but as a spiritual force. Honour, pride and independence constituted the concept of fatherland, which I perceived as an 'extension and aggrandisement of the ego'."

By the end of 1915 the gradual clarification of a new aesthetic led him to assert: "From the investigations I pursued, I reached the conclusion that naturalism had purged painting of its spiritual atmosphere."

Carrà was not alone in his ideas, sharing his reappraisal of history and artistic conventions with Soffici, de Chirico, Savinio and de Pisis. "Our still imperfect works, my dear friends Soffici and de Chirico, are nothing but the first buds to appear after an almost centuries-long thaw."

Apparitions, sparks of consciousness, spots of light in our everyday material surroundings: here are Carrà's intuitions. It is precisely in these "apparitions", in these essential "flashes of inspiration from ordinary things", that one can detect the most typical and original features of the artist's conception of the metaphysical – so different, in terms of both intellectual approach and pictorial depiction, from the composite and choreographic "mythographies" of de Chirico. Carrà's work painfully depicts a naked, true metaphysical solitude – a passkey to the other reality: the "mythical (though ordinary) reality" which despite having different features, was to be a constant in his work. "As the years went by, I remained faithful to this quest for a true poetic and a true metaphysics, consistently subordinating to this end the existence of the truly physical."

From "Valori Plastici" to Mythical Realism

"Once the War was over I had the idea of creating an artistic movement which would integrate the very best developments taking place in Italy; I was considering founding a journal which would have a revisionist and constructive character and be a point of contact between the new tendencies and personalities manifesting themselves in the sphere of the figurative arts."

In the spring of 1918 the painter and critic Mario Broglio was also organizing a new artistic journal in Rome, entitled *Valori Plastici*, that would unite painters, art historians and critics, and discuss, in the wake of the avant-garde experience, the codification of the new aesthetic values which were in the process of forming.

On 22 April 1918 de Chirico wrote to Carrà: "Dear Carrà. I find myself on leave in Rome. On 15 May the first number of a journal will come out: send a poem or a prose lyric. But be quick. It will be a serious review." Carrà accepted the invitation and sent Broglio a theoretical essay entitled *The quadrant of the spirit* (*Il quadrante dello spirito*).

For various reasons, the first number of the journal did not appear until 15 November 1918 and Carrà's text, which opened it, assumed the character of a manifesto for the review, or a statement of its objectives. In March 1919 Broglio wrote to Carrà: "I am happy to acknowledge it again: your contribution is essential, as it makes it possible to compile a survey capable of offering a true reflection of our pictorial activity here in Italy."

Naturally, the stance taken by Carrà and *Valori Plastici* found many opponents: "The most banal of our adversaries tell us we live in a spirit of extreme decadence... All things considered, if the artist's spirit has changed it has done so for the better."

However, Carrà's critical and expository ardour did not correspond to a pictorial fervour: between 1918 and 1920 he produced only three paintings and an indeterminate number of drawings. This was symptomatic of an inner aesthetic tension which, whilst finding resolution in theoretical texts, was unable to translate itself into visible form on the blank canvas. The fundamental problem remained the relationship between the artist and the external world of things – nature included, indeed foremost. Consequently, there arose a need for a new relationship between "reality and intellectual values". In 1921 Carrà began to perceive a solution: "I was attempting to recreate a mythical representation of nature... Such a vision, born of a long, dark gestation, signified for me the dawning of a great pictorial truth, almost entirely absent in the earlier phases of my work." Declarations such as these sound like the first words of someone lost at sea upon reaching the Promised Land. In the transition from metaphysical painting to mythical realism, Carrà stretches and tears asunder that veil which had previously only allowed us to glimpse our "parallel reality". If before we were only able to grasp "apparitions", now the vision is enlarged and nature, outside of any naturalistic longing, appears to us illuminated in a new light.

From this moment onward the mythical relationship with nature, and a transfigured vision of it, became a lietmotiv of pictorial representation for Carrà.

The process of identification with the object depicted – be it a landscape, a still life or figures in a natural setting – is not casual, but scientific, being dominated by an architectural construction of the artwork which is never forgotten or neglected.

This new pictorial aesthetic provoked much polemic from both friends and colleagues, as well as from the nascent "Novecento" group, which gravitated around the critic Margherita Sarfatti and which counted Sironi amongst its most prominent supporters. Sironi's firm committment was to not *elude* tradition, but rather to compete with it in its own domain, "merging the splendours of antiquity with vibrant modern aspirations".

In fact, in a gesture of opposition to the aesthetics of *Valori Plastici*, Sironi had adhered to the manifesto *Against all returns in painting* (*Contro tutti i ritorni in pittura*) which was first published by Luigi Russolo and reprinted in 1920.

To Carra's idea of a "return" – that is to say, imitation of the art of antiquity – Russolo, Sironi and companions opposed a pictorial construction which was not imitative of or inspired by the primitivism of the masters of the Trecento or Quattrocento, thereby revealing sensibilities still marked by the Futurist experience. "Others seek to couch this sterile and ponderous imitation in terms of a return to a healthy tradition, which in actual fact constitutes a facile, lazy retreat. We declare that the true Italian tradition is that of never having had any tradition, since the Italian race is one of innovators and constructors. Art history teaches us what mediocre results such returns in art have led to."

Carrà responded to this attack in 1925 in the following manner: "Since 1916 we have tried to re-establish the fundamental principles of the Italian tradition and many of those who today present themselves in the same light, as reconstructors of tradition, originally condemned our ideas, accusing us of cowardice and of injuring modernity… In fact, since May 1920 we have protested against their new infatuation and have tried to outline some observations capable of neutralizing the harm – as yet uncertain, but extremely symptomatic – which is being inflicted on Italian art in the name of tradition."

The polemics were to continue during these years due to Sironi's increasing concern that "landscape painting is an obstruction to the development of truly great figure painting".

A partial rapprochement was achieved with Sironi's invitation to Carrà, amongst others, to execute frescoes for the 5th Triennale, held in Milan in 1933.

Over the years, the misunderstandings and accusations led Carrà to constantly have to justify himself and explain an approach to painting which was highly singular, despite attracting disciples and having associations with certain schools of thought.

"I will only say", Carrà stated in his *Self-presentation* (*Autopresentazione*) of 1935, "that I consider my works to be the result of a spiritual tendency which has its goal in the re-establishment of that relationship of historical continuity and harmony between colour and form, a relationship which for my generation was ruptured… The supreme end of art is the sovereignty of universal sentiments. For this reason, the great artist is both an individuality and a plurality. Art thus passes from the individual to the collective, from the spirit of one man to that of all mankind."

The theoretical and mental praxis apparently falters only in contact with nature, and here it is as if the soul opens and a river completely breaches the dam of the intellect, in order that it might repose in simple contemplation: "Painting may be defined as a loving embrace of man and nature, a melancholia imbued with the blood of a heart."

Carlo Carrà
Works on Paper

Naval war in the Adriatic / *Guerra navale nell'Adriatico*, 1914-15
Pencil, ink and collage on card, 370 × 270 mm
Antonio and Marina Forchino collection, Turin

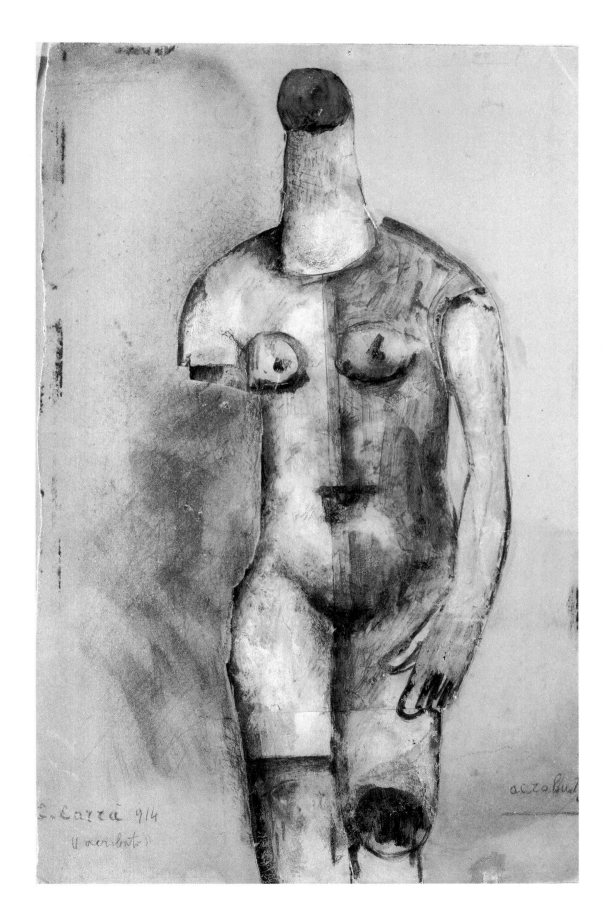

Acrobat / *Acrobata*, 1914
Collage and tempera on card, 390 × 240 mm
Private collection, Bergamo

The flask / *Il fiasco*, 1915
Tempera and collage, 395 × 315 mm
Private collection, Milan

Outskirts of Milan / *Periferia milanese*, 1909
Crayon on paper, 233 × 320 mm
Private collection, Milan

Head of a young girl / *Testa di fanciulla*, 1909
Pencil and charcoal on paper, 140 × 90 mm
Private collection, Milan

Ballerina, 1910
Crayon on paper, 200 × 145 mm
Private collection, Milan

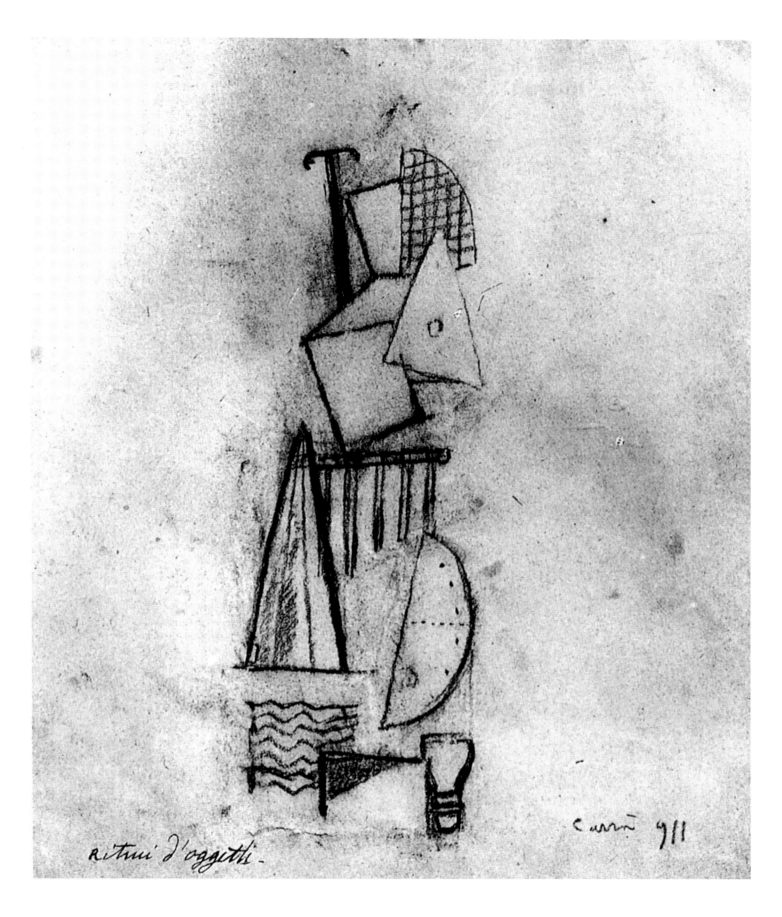

Rhythms of objects / *Ritmi di oggetti*, 1911
Charcoal on paper, 200 × 165 mm
Galleria Anna D'Ascanio, Rome

Fragmentation of a head / *Scomposizione di testa*, 1912
Ink on paper, 220 × 130 mm
Private collection, Milan

Head of a woman / *Testa di donna*, 1912
Ink on paper, 140 × 128 mm
Private collection, Milan

Fragmentation of a figure / *Scomposizione di figura*, 1912
Blue pencil on paper, 280 × 185 mm
Private collection, Milan

Still life / *Natura morta*, 1912
Ink on the reverse of a Futurist handbill, 158 × 128 mm
Private collection, Milan

The mistress's house / *La casa dell'amante*, c. 1912
Pencil on card, 110 × 68 mm
Private collection, Milan

Women / *Donne*, 1914
Ink on paper, 115 × 143 mm
Private collection, Milan

Ballerina, 1913
Ink on paper, 186 × 112 mm
Galleria Anna D'Ascanio, Rome

Nude / *Nudo*, 1914
Watercolour on paper, 305 × 165 mm
Galleria Anna D'Ascanio, Rome

The house of love / *La casa dell'amore*, 1914
Pencil on paper, 200 × 125 mm
Galleria Anna D'Ascanio, Rome

Penelope (The idol) / *Penelope (L'idolo)*, 1914
Crayon on paper, 1130 × 475 mm
Galleria Anna D'Ascanio, Rome

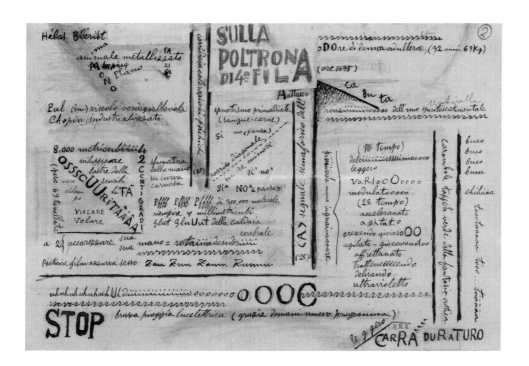

Cinelove / *Cineamore*, 1914
Ink on paper, 272 × 376 mm
Private collection, Milan

Marine vision / *Visione marina*, 1914
Crayon on paper, 155 × 105 mm
Private collection, Milan

Half-length figure / *Mezza figura*, 1914
Pencil on paper, 186 × 110 mm
Private collection, Milan

Apollinaire, 1914
Crayon on paper, 200 × 183 mm
Private collection, Milan

Acrobat / *Acrobata*, 1914
Pencil on paper, 220 × 140 mm
Private collection, Milan

Solitude / *Solitudine*, 1914
Pencil on paper, 210 × 157 mm
Private collection, Rome

Figures in a landscape / *Figure in un paesaggio*, 1915
Pencil on paper, 200 × 190 mm
Private collection, Milan

The child prodigy / *Il fanciullo prodigio*, 1914
Pencil on paper, 265 × 196 mm
Private collection, Reggio Emilia

Men II / *Uomini II*, 1915
Pencil on paper, 230 × 185 mm
Private collection, Milan

Prisoners of war / *Prigionieri di guerra*, 1915
Ink on paper, 235 × 150 mm
Private collection, Milan

Field gun towed at full gallop / *Cannone trainato al galoppo*, 1915
Pencil on paper, 163 × 230 mm
Private collection, Milan

War flight (Large bombs) / *Volo di guerra (Bomboni)*, 1915
Pencil on paper, 140 × 195 mm
Private collection, Milan

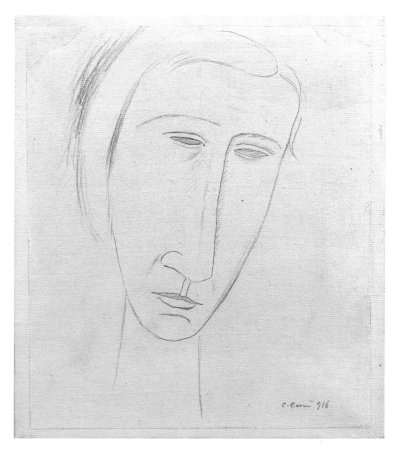

Portrait / *Ritratto*, 1916
Pencil on paper, 282 × 230 mm
Private collection, Turin

At La Scala / *Alla Scala*, 1915
Pencil on paper, 144 × 102 mm
Private collection, Milan

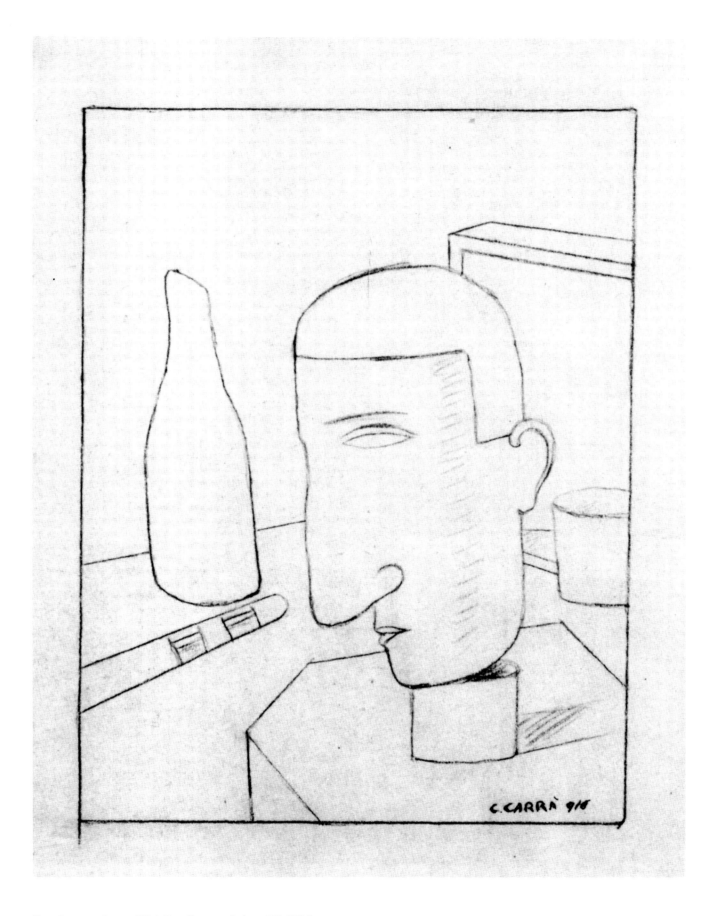

Drunken gentleman III / *Gentiluomo ubriaco III*, 1916
Pencil on lined paper, 355 × 280 mm
Private collection, Bergamo

Mannequin / *Manichino*, 1916
Pencil on paper, 414 × 325 mm
Galleria Anna D'Ascanio, Rome

Mad poet / *Poeta folle*, 1916
Charcoal on paper, 360 × 260 mm
Galleria Pegaso, Forte dei Marmi

Mad poet II / *Poeta folle II*, 1916
Crayon on paper, 170 × 140 mm
Private collection, Rome

Mad poet / *Poeta folle*, c. 1916
Pencil on paper, 297 × 207 mm
Private collection, Milan

Head of a gentleman III / *Testa di gentiluomo III*, 1916
Crayon and ink on paper, 305 × 190 mm
Private collection, Reggio Emilia

The carriage / *La carrozzella*, 1916
Pencil on paper, 215 × 270 mm
Private collection, Milan

Angel II / *Angelo II*, 1917
Indian ink on paper, 270 × 210 mm
Fondazione Antonio Mazzotta, Milan

Dice player / *Giocatore di dadi*, 1917
Ink on paper, 123 × 183 mm
Private collection, Rome

Dice player / *Giocatore di dadi*, 1917
Pencil on paper, 180 × 260 mm
Private collection, Milan

Magical room / *Camera magica*, 1917
Pencil on paper, 280 × 213 mm
Private collection, Milan

Two mannequins / *Due manichini*, 1917
Pencil on paper, 214 × 160 mm
Galleria La Scaletta, Reggio Emilia

The two sisters / *Le due sorelle*, 1917
Crayon on paper, 180 × 125 mm
Private collection, Milan

Objects in the square / *Oggetti nella piazza*, 1917
Charcoal on paper, 215 × 152 mm
Galleria La Scaletta, Reggio Emilia

Mannequin / *Manichino*, 1917
Ink and watercolour on card, 410 × 255 mm
Private collection, Milan

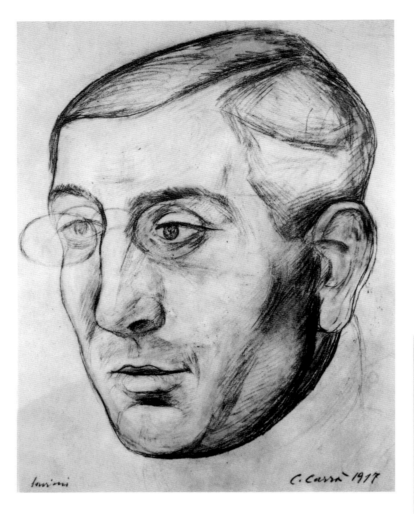

Savinio, 1917
Pencil on paper, 275 × 205 mm
Private collection, Rome

Metaphysical mannequin / *Manichino metafisico*, c. 1918
Pencil on paper, 150 × 105 mm
Private collection, Rome

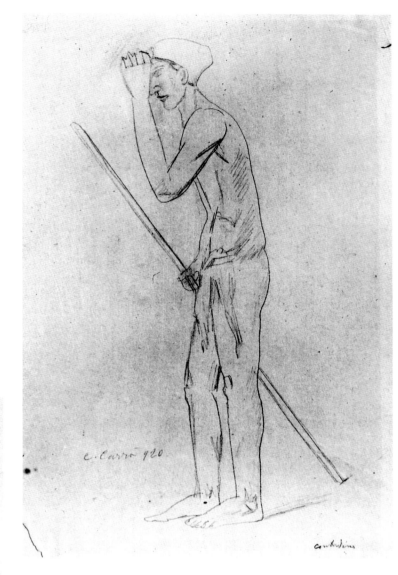

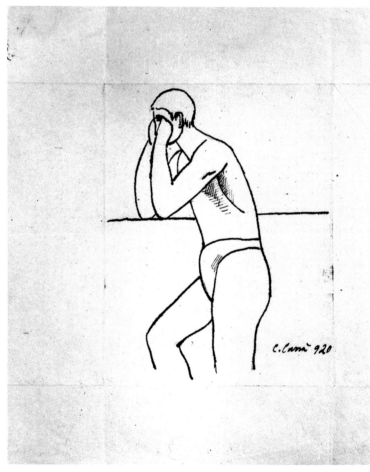

Meditation / *Meditazione*, 1920
Ink on paper, 282 × 220 mm
Galleria Anna D'Ascanio, Rome

Peasant / *Contadino*, 1920
Pencil on paper, 320 × 222 mm
Private collection, Milan

The Dioscuri / *I Dioscuri*, 1920
Pencil on paper, 200 × 175 mm
Private collection, Milan

The traveller III / *Il viandante III*, 1921
Charcoal on paper, 580 × 400 mm
Private collection, Bologna

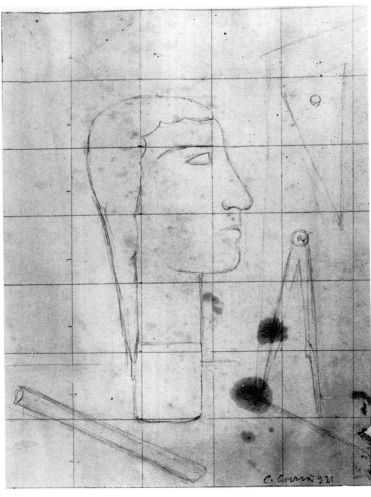

The engineer's mistress III / *L'amante dell'ingegnere III*, 1921
Pencil on paper, 280 × 210 mm
Galleria Anna D'Ascanio, Rome

The engineer's mistress I / *L'amante dell'ingegnere I*, 1921
Pencil on paper, 148 × 110 mm
Private collection, Milan

The fisherman's house / *La casa del pescatore*, 1921
Pencil on paper, 160 × 215 mm
Galleria La Scaletta, Reggio Emilia

The brawl / *La rissa*, 1921
Pencil on paper, 175 × 225 mm
Galleria La Scaletta, Reggio Emilia

The house of love / *La casa dell'amore*, 1922
Pencil on paper, 280 × 220 mm
Galleria Anna D'Ascanio, Rome

Bust of a child / *Busto di bambino*, 1921
Pencil on paper, 200 × 195 mm
Antonio and Marina Forchino collection, Turin

Twilight / *Crepuscolo*, 1922
Pencil on paper, 360 × 520 mm
Private collection, Milan

Mother and daughter / *Madre e figlia*, 1922
Ink on paper, 285 × 225 mm
Private collection, Milan

The lovers / *Gli amanti*, 1922
Pencil on paper, 210 × 300 mm
Galleria Anna D'Ascanio, Rome

The lovers / *Gli amanti*, 1925
Pencil on paper, 275 × 330 mm
Private collection, Milan

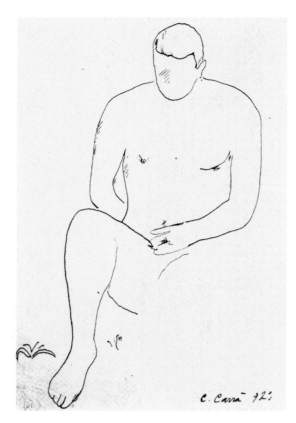

Figure / *Figura*, 1923
Ink on paper, 275 × 185 mm
Private collection, Milan

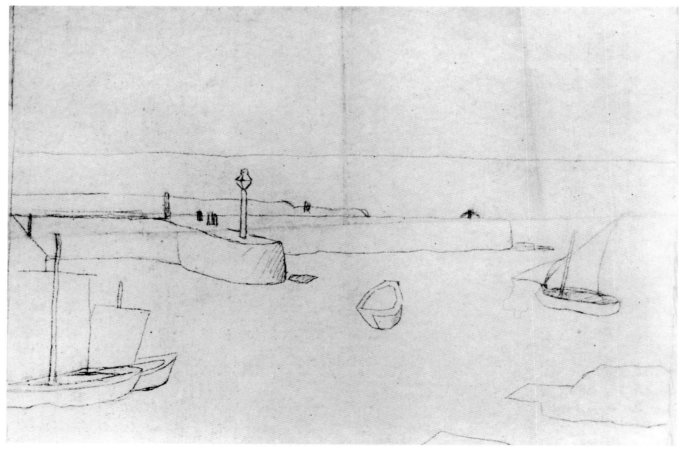

The harbour of Camogli / *Il porto di Camogli*, 1923
Pencil on paper, 512 × 745 mm
Galleria Anna D'Ascanio, Rome

Female figure / *Figura femminile*, 1933
Pencil on paper, 280 × 220 mm
Private collection, Milan

Self-portrait / *Autoritratto*, 1929
Tempera and pencil on card, 265 × 215 mm
Private collection, Milan

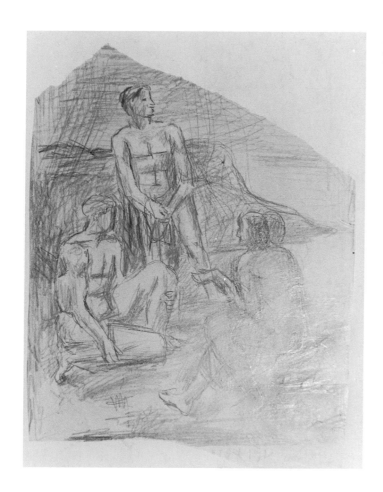

Fishermen / *Pescatori*, 1931
Pencil on paper, 255 × 200 mm
Private collection, Milan

Women by the sea II / *Donne al mare II*, 1931
Crayon on paper, 206 × 237 mm
Private collection, Milan

Astrid, 1945
Pencil on paper, 294 × 195 mm
Galleria La Scaletta, Reggio Emilia

Two women / *Due donne*, 1945
Ink on paper, 310 × 215 mm
Private collection, Milan

In the harbour of Barcelona / *Nella rada di Barcellona*, 1945
Pencil on paper, 400 × 279 mm
Private collection, Milan

Faun and young girl / *Fauno e fanciulla*, 1949
Watercolour on paper, 227 × 163 mm
Private collection, Milan

Seated woman / *Donna seduta*, 1965
Pencil on paper, 480 × 330 mm
Private collection, Milan

Woman with a book / *Donna con il libro*, 1952
Charcoal on paper, 410 × 293 mm
Private collection, Reggio Emilia

Brief Notes on Carrà's Mural Painting

Renato Miracco

"The drawing precedes the work on a summarizing basis, open to modifications... The spirit determines the concrete reality. Our obstinate demand is that of ensuring the drawing precedes the reconstruction of the painting, which happens architectonically, not casually. Once the law has been discovered, one can apply it to individual cases."

If this conviction of Carrà's is manifested throughout his oeuvre, it is particularly relevant to the preparatory drawings and studies relating to his mural works, the most important examples of which were those created for the 5th Triennale of 1933, the 6th Triennale of 1936 and the Palazzo di Giustizia in Milan, executed between 1938 and 1939. "My intention in these works", Carrà stated in his autobiography, referring to his frescoes for the Palazzo di Giustizia, "was to adhere to a simple and clear method and to endow the forms with a fluid, chromatic transparency, which would not detract from the firmness of the volumes, so as to achieve an ease of comprehension."

Besides Carrà, Sironi – as director – had invited the most prominent artists of the day, such as de Chirico, Casorati, Campigli, Funi, Severini, Prampolini and Andreotti, amongst others, to fresco the walls at the 5th Triennale. As early as 1931 Carrà had agreed to Sironi's offer and had begun to work on the theme assigned to him: *Life in Roman Italy* (*Vita nell'Italia romana*), a title which was shortened to just *Roman Italy* in the final version.

In an article of 1932 in *Il Popolo d'Italia* Sironi proposed that what captured Carrà's imagination was "not simply the pure enlargement of works across great expanses, but new problems of spatiality, of form, of expression and of lyrical, epic or dramatic content. One perceives a renovation of rhythms, of equilibriums, of a constructive spirit, in which there could return, for art, those values which the triumph of nineteenth century Nordic realism had destroyed".

This new adventure was to lead Carrà, together with Campigli and Funi, to sign the *Manifesto of mural painting* (*Manifesto della pittura murale*), written by Sironi in 1933: "The individualist conception of 'art for art's sake' is dead... Modern painting today feels the need for a superior spiritual synthesis... A moral question arises for every artist. He must renounce his egocentricity and become a militant artist who serves a moral ideal, subordinating his own individuality to collective work."

Following this principle, in his first mural – measuring four by nine metres, now destroyed – Carrà aimed to represent a Roman society regulated by very precise principles, not only of a religious order but also of a civil kind. The fresco, which can be studied today through photographic documentation and preparatory studies, was the fruit of a laborious compositional process involving numerous modifications and substitutions. It depicts the working life since the dawn of mankind, moving from the condition of humanity in the Stone Age to the depiction of shepherds – the first stage of economic evolution – before passing to images of navigators, symbolic of commercial activity.

The lower section depicts men building a temple – that is to say, humanity laying the foundations of modern society. A restless horse appears at the centre, symbolizing primitive force, surrounded by various figures of allegorical significance.

In 1936 Carrà, like almost all the other artists, chose to present works on canvas which were then affixed to the walls, rather than to work directly on them. This was done in order to avoid their being obliterated and because the technique which he employed did not itself guarantee longevity. Carrà painted three canvases, each measuring two by three metres, representing the *Marble industry* (*Industria del marmo*), a subject freely inspired by work at the caves of Massa Carrara. Unfortunately, the works were destroyed and one can therefore only refer to the existing photographic documentation.

The frescoes for the Palazzo di Giustizia in Milan are the only surviving examples of Carrà's mural art. From an analysis of the preparatory drawings and cartoons for both *Justinian freeing the slave* (*Giustiniano libera lo schiavo*) and *The Last Judgement* (*Giudizio finale*) one can observe how Carrà deliberately and systematically eliminated figures, symbols and emblems in order to consistently obey his principles of clarity and ease of reading. Both frescoes, dedicated to the theme of human and divine justice, were censored due to the presence of nude figures. Carrà's decision to favour the nude was motivated by an attempt to attain a harmony between form and content, between the social function of art and the requirements of the creative language.

Of the two frescoes, *Justinian freeing the slave* is certainly the one most strongly indebted to the art of the Renaissance, being strongly bound by its compositional structure to Italian pictorial tradition, to Giotto, Masaccio and Paolo Uccello. This assertion is justified, in the first place, by the integration of architecture and landscape typical of Renaissance art. "Having established the colouristic and formal values, I will add", wrote Carrà, "that the use of the golden section and the rules of squares, triangles, diagonals and the Cross of St Andrea also proved very useful to me in the composition of the work with regard to both the figure and the landscape. Thus the number re-entered my painting – that is to say, the harmonic division of planes and spaces, as was manifested by Paolo Uccello and Piero della Francesca in their paintings."

The Last Judgement is a fresco I would venture to call atypical. As has been recently observed, it is in this mural more than any other that one perceives the transposition of standard pictorial conventions, matured by the artist, into a different and foreign context. Were it not for the figure of Christ, the entire scene could evoke any of the works typical of those years. Not by accident do *Boys by the sea* (*Ragazzi al mare*) of 1939 and *Bathing sailors* (*Bagno di marinai*) re-employ the same diagonal compositional structure. Moreover, in the oil *The Last Judgement* (*Giudizio universale*) – dated as a study to 1937 but as a completed work to 1947 – Carrà eliminates the figure of Christ, definitively divesting the painting of an allegorical-Christian character and again leading it back to a theme typical of those years but certainly not religious in the strict sense.

Regarding this matter, Carrà explained in a text of 1933 entitled *In favour of a modern sacred art* (*Per un'arte sacra moderna*) how religious painting ("social art *par excellence*") cannot exist if it does not overcome "in itself the restrictions of *contenutismo** and succeed in attaining a synthesis between content and form, in expressing values of a spiritual order".

Reassessing his time as a mural painter in his autobiography, Carrà concludes: "I do not delude myself at the present time with regard to these prevalently social pictorial manifestations, because it is very evident that the current climate is not propitious. Nevertheless, I nurture great faith in this particular application of figurative art. Perhaps one day mural painting – by which I understand not only fresco but encaustic, mosaic and various other techniques – will be able to rediscover its past splendour and recapture that breadth of conception which has always distinguished it down the ages. From 1940 onwards my easel painting has continued with rigour and assiduousness..."

* Strong emphasis upon the literary or anecdotal content of works of visual art.

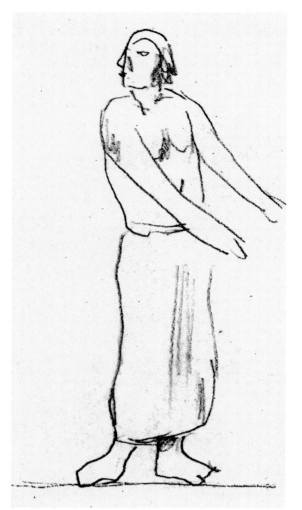

40 preparatory drawings
for the frescoes in Milan's
Palazzo di Giustizia (Law Courts),
1935-38
Pencil on paper,
various dimensions
Private collection, Milan

Figure study / *Studio di figura*, 1933 (c. 1932),
275 × 189 mm

Figure study / *Studio di figura*, 1931 (c. 1932),
180 × 80 mm

Brawl between statues and models / *Rissa fra statue
e modelli*, 1929
Pencil on paper, 206 × 140 mm
Galleria Anna D'Ascanio, Rome

Man ascending / *Uomo che sale*, 1927 (c. 1932),
277 × 222 mm

Composition / *Composizione*, 1932, 245 × 185 mm

Figure study / *Studio di figure*, 1932, 180 × 200 mm

The builders of the temple (The ancestry) / *I costruttori del tempio (La stirpe)*, 1933, 370 × 215 mm

The builders of the temple / *I costruttori del tempio*, c. 1932, 160 × 265 mm

The builders of the temple / *I costruttori del tempio*, c. 1932, 150 × 265 mm

Study for a fresco / *Studio di affresco*, 1932, 223 × 275 mm

The builders of the temple / *I costruttori del tempio*, c. 1932,
205 × 735 mm

The builders of the temple / *I costruttori del tempio*, 1933,
365 × 180 mm

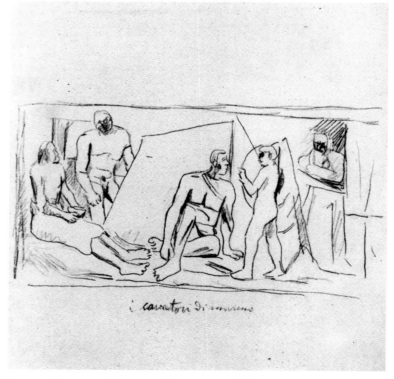

The marble cutters / *I cavatori di marmo*, c. 1932,
210 × 280 mm

Cain and Abel. Slavery freed /
Caino e Abele. La schiavitù liberata, 1934,
200 × 220 mm

Cain and Abel and Justice /
Caino e Abele e la Giustizia, 1933,
205 × 280 mm

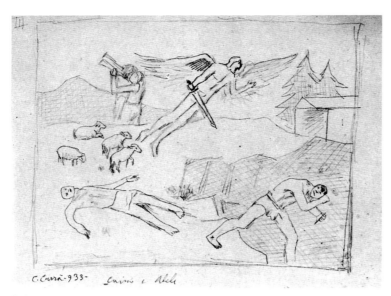

Cain and Abel / *Caino e Abele*, 1933, 220 × 285 mm

Law brings order to human society / *La legge porta l'ordine
all'umana società*, 1934-35, 222 × 284 mm

Rome brings order to human society / *Roma porta l'ordine
alla società umana*, 1934-35, 205 × 196 mm

Justice frees the slaves and punishes the sinner / *La Giustizia libera gli schiavi
e punisce il delitto*, 1935, 200 × 215 mm

Slavery liberated and Sin punished by Justice inspired by Law / *La Schiavitù liberata e il Delitto punito dalla Giustizia ispirata dal Diritto*, 1934-35, 222 × 284 mm

Law defends the righteous and punishes the sinners / *La legge difende i buoni e punisce i cattivi*, 1935, 222 × 284 mm

Justice frees the slave and punishes the sinner / *La Giustizia libera lo schiavo e punisce il delitto*, 1935, 284 × 222 mm

Justinian / *Giustiniano*, 1935, 205 × 185 mm

Justinian / *Giustiniano*, 1935, 185 × 190 mm

Roman Justice / *La Giustizia romana*, c. 1935, 222 × 284 mm

Justinian carriyng the new code to the Roman Empire
/ *Giustiniano reca il nuovo codice all'Impero Romano*,
1934-35, 220 × 284 mm

Justinian / *Giustiniano*, 1934, 180 × 195 mm

Justinian / *Giustiniano*, 1935, 205 × 225 mm

Justinian / *Giustiniano*, 1935, 190 × 210 mm

Justice / *La Giustizia*, 1934-35, 230 × 277 mm

Justinian / *Giustiniano*, c. 1934-35, 222 × 283 mm

Roman legislative genius / *Il genio legislativo romano*,
1938, 222 × 283 mm

Justinian / *Giustiniano*, 1935-38, 105 × 103 mm

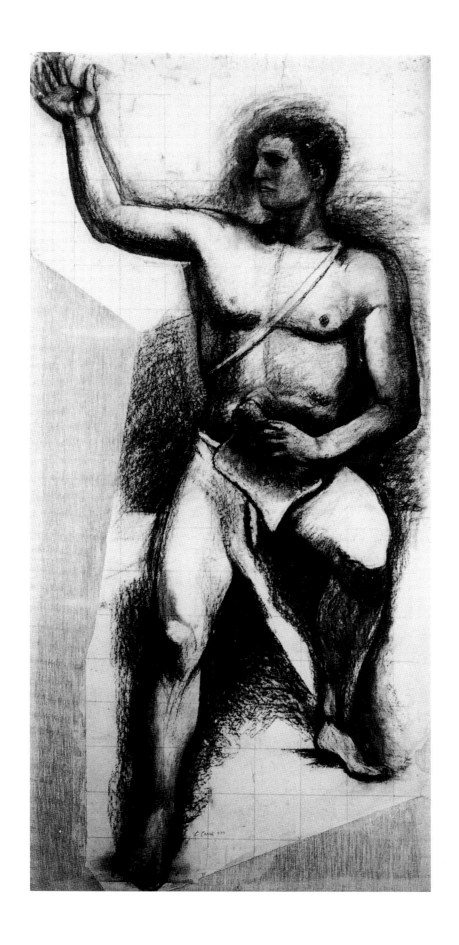

Preparatory charcoal study for *Justinian*, c. 1938
Charcoal on yellow paper, 2740 × 1300 mm

Justinian / *Giustiniano*, c. 1934-35, 222 × 283 mm

Justinian / *Giustiniano*, c. 1935-38, 237 × 350 mm

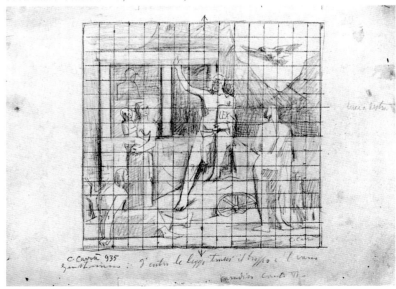

Justinian / *Giustiniano*, c. 1935-38, 240 × 350 mm

The Last Judgment / *Giudizio finale*, c. 1935, 237 × 350 mm

The Last Judgment / *Giudizio finale*, 1938, 240 × 350 mm

The Last Judgment / *Giudizio finale*, c. 1938, 238 × 350 mm

The Last Judgment / *Giudizio finale*,
1935, 222 × 284 mm

The Last Judgment / *Giudizio finale*,
1935-38, 222 × 225 mm

23255 Dawsons £8·96—

Finito di stampare nel settembre 2001
presso le Arti Grafiche Salea di Milano
per conto delle Edizioni Gabriele Mazzotta